LOUIS
ARMSTRONG

Mason Crest Publishers, Inc.
370 Reed Road
Broomall, Pennsylvania 19008
866-MCP-BOOK (toll free)

Illustrations copyright © 2000 Francois Roca
Published in association with
Grimm Press Ltd., Taiwan
Printed in Taiwan.

1 3 5 7 9 8 6 4 2

Library of Congress Cataloging-in-
Publication Data:

on file at the Library of Congress.
ISBN 1-59084-135-2
ISBN 1-59084-133-6 (series)

Great Names

LOUIS
ARMSTRONG

Mason Crest Publishers

Philadelphia

This book is about Louis Armstrong, the Father of Jazz. But what is jazz?

Jazz is a rich form of music that didn't exist 100 years ago. Its roots stretch back to the days of slavery in America. Beginning in the 1600s, black people were taken from their homes in Africa. They were shipped to North America and sold as slaves to labor on farms.

Though far from home and without freedom, the slaves clung to their traditions, especially music. Over the centuries, the African culture merged with European instruments and music to give birth to jazz. The music of slaves, which they used to remember their loved ones and express their sorrow, would become one of the most popular forms of 20th-century music.

New Orleans was an exciting place to be at the beginning of the 1900s. Immigrants from all over Europe, as well as many freed slaves, settled there. The city pulsed with the music of many cultures and traditions. New Orleans was full of opera troupes, orchestras, and bands. Parades filed down the streets. Bands and dancers performed in the parks. Though most people in New Orleans didn't know it, the sounds of jazz were already a part of their lives.

Louis Armstrong was born in New Orleans on August 4, 1901. His father left when Louis was still a young child, but Louis never missed him. His mother, grandmother, and sister were all the family he needed. Louis grew up very poor, and his mother struggled to make ends meet. When the hunger became too great, Louis rummaged through garbage tins for scraps. He rarely found anything because his neighbors were just as poor.

When Louis grew older, he discovered a way to earn his food—by performing. With a group of friends, he danced and sang on street corners, hoping a passerby would reward their performance with a coin or two. The boys earned many meals this way.

Louis often went to outdoor band performances. He loved the passionate music so much it would make him forget his hunger. Dancing and swaying to the beat, he would dream of the day he would own a trumpet and play this wonderful music.

At the age of 13, Louis's life suddenly changed. On New Year's Eve in 1913, Louis mixed with the crowds of people celebrating in the streets. The air was filled with fireworks, music, and excitement. Louis wanted to join the fun. He took his mother's gun from her trunk and fired six shots into the air. Although no one was hurt, the police took him away the next day and sent him to a reform school.

Getting locked up in reform school was a harsh punishment, but it did give Louis a great opportunity—his first music lessons. Even better, the reform school had an orchestra. Louis jumped at the chance to join it. He was first told to play the cymbals, not his beloved trumpet.

But his teacher quickly noticed that Louis had an excellent feel for rhythm. Louis couldn't read music, but he could remember any tune he heard. His teacher began to coach Louis and found he was a natural musician.

When Louis left the reform school a year and a half later, his teacher gave him a parting gift—a trumpet! Louis's first dream had come true.

When Louis was 17 years old, he met Kid Ory, a great jazzman. Louis joined Ory's band. Although only an assistant, Louis played his trumpet along with the band whenever he could. Ory became Louis's friend and family, and from him Louis learned the basics of jazz.

When Ory left New Orleans to play jazz in Chicago, Louis became the leader of Ory's band. The dedicated student had become a true jazz musician at last. Four years later, Ory asked Louis to join him in Chicago. Louis went eagerly.

Louis played better and better, until he even surpassed his old teacher Ory. Louis developed a new style of playing called improvisation. Instead of playing a tune as it was written, he would break off in the middle and add something of his own invention, giving an entirely new feel to the song. Today, improvisation is one of the things people love most about jazz. It makes a piece of music sound fresh and new each time it's played.

Louis's reputation spread and he was invited to join a jazz group in New York City. The city was a new world to Louis. The musicians dressed smart and liked to have a good time. They spent their money freely in bars and clubs. Compared to them, Louis was a country bumpkin. He didn't care about his appearance, didn't drink much, and saved most of his money.

In the beginning, the other band members were cool toward him and looked down on him. They were wary of this newcomer and potential competitor. But, like so many others, they were soon won over by his warmth and amazing creativity. He added spark and energy to the band. Later they nicknamed him "satchel mouth"—or Satchmo—because of his constant broad smile.

the HOT FIVE

In 1925, Louis returned to Chicago to organize his own band, the Hot Five. Louis's playing in New York had attracted attention, and several well-known musicians eagerly accepted invitations to join the band.

Over the next two years, the band recorded an incredible 23 records, all of them still admired by jazz fans today. In addition to playing the trumpet, Louis sang. He created a new musical language, called *scat*.

In scat, the words sung are not real words, just sounds. He turned the voice into an instrument, exploring every sound possible for the mouth to make. The freedom of this style allowed the singer to express more emotions. Today, scat is a fundamental part of jazz.

Not everyone was convinced that Louis was a great player.
Several excellent trumpet players from the Boston Symphony Orchestra,
for example, doubted his genius. They decided to visit Louis in his
dressing room and see for themselves.

Louis played for them. He began with the tune they suggested,
but soon broke into an improvisation that left the visitors shaking
their heads in wonder.

"I was watching his fingers closely," said one, "but I still couldn't
see how he did it. It's extraordinary how just one person can create a
sound like a whole band!"

In June 1931, Louis returned to New Orleans for the first time in nearly 10 years. As the train pulled into the station, a torrent of music greeted him. Eight jazz bands were lined up along the platform, playing a welcome. The crowd went crazy with excitement when he appeared. Lifting him onto their shoulders, they carried him through streets decorated with "Welcome home, Louis" signs. They passed a shop named after him and a baseball team wearing uniforms with his name stitched across the front.

Louis performed in New Orleans for three months, but the clubs only seated white people. Black fans were forced to stand outside windows or tune to the radio to hear him. Not only the fans experienced racism; so did Louis. During the first broadcast, the white announcer suddenly said he would not introduce a black man. Louis had to rush to the microphone and introduce himself.

Not everything went easy for Louis. Like other artists, he had an agent—a person who managed his schedule and money. But his agent didn't do his job well. He booked Louis to play so many concerts that Louis damaged his lips. They never fully recovered. Louis was forced to rely on medicine to ease the pain.

The worst damage occurred in a concert in November 1932. Louis blew high notes, putting enormous pressure on his lips. They split and began to bleed. But Louis struggled on to the end of the song, the blood running down his neck, chest, and to his knees.

By the time Louis replaced his agent, he had serious money problems. He owed several years in taxes and was deeply in debt.

Then, in the 1930s, the American economy collapsed. Bars closed, making it hard for musicians to find work. To add to Louis's difficulties, some music critics complained that Louis had become just an entertainer and was no longer a true jazz musician. Louis didn't take this to heart. He just wanted to make audiences happy and express his emotions in music.

Louis found himself a new and better agent. His new agent swiftly solved Louis's financial problems and rebuilt his career. At his suggestion, Louis took his band on a tour of the southern, central, and western states.

At that time, black and white people were separated by laws. For a black man, traveling in the South was difficult. Even finding a place to eat and sleep presented problems. The hotels were often for whites only. This meant the band had to sleep on buses or rent cheap rooms. They ate meals of bread and canned food.

Even more difficult, when the bus pulled into a rest stop, the doors were quickly locked. Louis was a famous musician, but he was treated like any other black man.

At 42, Louis married for the fourth and final time, to Lucy. Having spent most of his life on the road, sleeping in trains, buses, and hotels, Louis would soon understand what it was to have a home of his own.

A year after they were married, Lucy bought a small house in Queens, New York. Louis was away on tour at the time and he wasn't happy when he heard the news. He was used to renting, and he didn't like the idea of being too settled.

When the tour ended and he returned to New York, Louis called Lucy from the bus station. If he didn't like the place, he said, he would turn around and walk straight out. When the taxis pulled up to the house, he told the driver to wait. He knocked on the door and Lucy cheerfully welcomed him home. Louis looked the place over from top to bottom, inside and out. But Lucy not only had arranged everything perfectly, she had cooked a marvelous dinner. Louis fell in love with the place. He invited the taxi driver to come in and eat, and they all sat down happily to dinner.

This was Louis's first and last real home. Even though he bought a mansion some years later, he continued to live in this small house.

Jazz became immensely popular during World War II. Americans all over the country listened to it. But after the war, Americans' passion for jazz faded, and the big bands lost their popularity. A new music called Rock 'n' Roll began to take over. Louis decided to put together a small jazz group that would combine the more traditional New Orleans sound with the big band one. The experiment was a success.

Starting in 1948, Louis and his band began to tour overseas. Although they were welcomed wherever they went, Louis found his trip to Africa and Ghana most moving. Ghana was the country of his ancestors and the source of jazz.

Louis charmed audiences and his music won America many fans. The *New York Times* called him "America's secret weapon." *Time* magazine put him on its cover. In 1960, the American government sponsored a tour to Africa. Louis and the band returned to Ghana and performed 45 concerts in 11 countries. The African musicians gave him a name: Okuka Lokole, one who charms beasts with music.

At age 60, Louis's health started to trouble him, though he remained as passionate about jazz as ever. In 1963, he wrote and performed the song "Hello Dolly." The recording was a great success and sold thousands of copies. In 1968, he recorded the famous "It's a Wonderful World."

In the following years, Louis's health worsened. He was often in the hospital, but he refused to give up performing or recording. In March 1971, his doctors feared he might collapse on stage. They told him to cancel his concerts.

"You don't understand," he replied. "My life, my soul, my spirit, is playing the trumpet. The concerts are arranged. The audience is expecting me. I can't let them down."

In July, after two weeks of treatment, he was released to go home and rest. But he felt so much better that he attended a rehearsal. He died the next morning in his sleep.

Louis was often asked what he thought about when he improvised. "As soon as I close my eyes," he said, "I start to recall the wonderful times in my childhood and the music just starts to flow. To me jazz is a kind of happiness. You have to love it to play it."

Louis's life was full of difficulties and challenges. But he met them all with a big, warm grin. He loved the world and he lived his life fully. The words of his most famous song, "It's a Wonderful World," seem to say it all.

BIOGRAPHY

Brendan January was born and raised in Pleasantville, New York. After graduating from Haverford College in 1995, January earned his master's degree from Columbia Graduate School of Journalism. January is an award-winning writer of juvenile nonfiction and is currently a journalist at the *Philadelphia Inquirer*. He lives with his wife in New Jersey.